SAFER @ HOME WITH PFSENSE®

RECIPES TO SECURE YOUR HOME AND FAMILY'S INTERNET EXPERIENCE

MICHAEL LINES

2nd Edition 2024

ISBN: 978-1-964431-04-8 (non-KDP ebook)

ISBN: 978-1-964431-05-5 (non-KDP paperback)

ISBN: 979-8-666197-48-6 (KDP paperback)

Cover design and photo from Canva.com

For my wife, Deborah, for her boundless patience and support of all my endeavors.

Wisdom consists in being able to distinguish among dangers and make a choice of the least harmful.

NICCOLO MACHIAVELLI, THE PRINCE

INTRODUCTION

This book is intended for technically inclined individuals who want to protect their security and privacy from internet-related threats. The protection that consumer-grade routers or WiFi access points provide is often limited at best. In many cases, these products are nothing more than primitive routers doing network address translation (NAT) to hide the devices on the individual's local network devices from the internet. The functionality of these devices is limited, their performance is abysmal, and their security is even worse.[1] When vulnerabilities are detected in these products, the purchaser is unlikely to be informed of their existence, assuming the vendor even bothers to release a patch.[2]

---

1. *Router Bugs Flaws Hacks and Vulnerabilities*. (2016). Routersecurity.org. https://routersecurity.org/bugs.php
2. Riley, D. (2020, July 7). *Study finds home routers unpatched and full of known vulnerabilities*. SiliconANGLE. https://siliconangle.com/2020/07/06/study-finds-home-routers-unpatched-full-known-vulnerabilities/

There are alternatives that provide true business-grade capabilities for the more hands-on individual and that do not cost an arm and a leg. These are the software and hardware appliances from Netgate. Netgate's pfSense® is the industry leader in open-source firewall software, with over 1 million deployments worldwide to consumers, businesses, educational institutions, and governments. An active and free online support community is available to help individuals configure and use the pfSense software,[3] as well as paid support and professional services available for businesses.

In this book, I will describe how to set up Netgate's SG-1100 appliance to secure a typical consumer (or small business) network.[4] While my recommendations assume that you have an SG-1100 appliance, these recipes are just as applicable to any other Netgate appliance or even your own firewall if you have built it using an old PC and the free pfSense community edition software.[5]

HOW THIS BOOK IS STRUCTURED

This book is organized as a series of "recipes", where each chapter (recipe) solves a particular security or privacy problem. After you have set up your SG-1100 following the instructions under "Chapter 1 - The basic ingredients", which recipe you choose to apply next is up to you based on your needs. If a recipe depends on another recipe being performed first, I will let you know.

---

3. https://forum.netgate.com
4. https://shop.netgate.com/products/1100-pfsense
5. https://www.pfsense.org/download/

ABOUT THE SG-1100

The SG-1100 is Netgate's lowest-end appliance, yet even at that, it still delivers more performance than most consumer-grade routers. It is compact, silent, and power-efficient, and for internet connections up to around 500 Megabits per second (Mbs), it will be all that you need. Please note, that if you are running a gigabit fiber connection into your home, or if you wish to run more packages than are described in this book, you will need to upgrade to a more powerful appliance in Netgate's product line, or build your firewall using the pfSense community edition software.

Out of the box, the SG-1100, with a basic NAT configuration, is far ahead of most consumer-grade routers in terms of performance and security capabilities. If you are worried that the SG-1100 is not powerful enough, rest assured that it can support all the recipes in this book concurrently as long as your connection speed is not above the limit mentioned above.

WHO THIS BOOK IS FOR

This book is for those familiar with IP networking who like to get their hands dirty and experiment. If this is not you, don't feel bad, as this describes most electronics buyers.

In that case, as insufficient as I believe it to be, a good consumer router is your best choice. My recommendation for anyone in this case is to look at the products from Eero.[6] While Eero's products have nowhere near the capabilities of pfSense as firewalls or routers, for most consumers, they are plug-and-play

---

6. https://eero.com

and will serve their needs better than most consumer-level alternatives.

COMMAND CONVENTIONS

There are many configuration options in pfSense, and in this book, we will just be scratching the surface of what you can do. To understand what you need to do to execute my instructions, I will use the following convention when I describe navigation within pfSense and when entering information.

Navigation within the pfSense webpage will follow the convention of: **<Top Menubar Item> / <Sub Menu Item from Dropdown> / <Option on page>**. For example, if I want you to go to the firewall rules page to enter a particular rule for the WAN interface, I will show the navigation path you need to follow as **Firewall / Rules / WAN**.

Once you are on a pfSense page and I need you to either enter information, click a button or select an option in a field, I will refer to the item on the page by displaying it in bold, for example, **Bandwidth**. I will show the information or option I want you to enter into that field in quotes, such as "100". Enter the information without the quotes.

A FINAL WORD OF WARNING

I ASSUME NO LIABILITY FOR ANY COSTS OR DAMAGES THAT MAY OCCUR FROM YOUR FOLLOWING (OR NOT FOLLOWING) THE INSTRUCTIONS IN THIS BOOK, OR FOR ANY ERRORS IN THESE INSTRUCTIONS. IF YOU DON'T UNDERSTAND IT, DON'T DO IT.

While all my advice in this book regarding configurations is based on my personal experience with my SG-1100, since I am not there configuring your device, I cannot guarantee your success. Likewise, I cannot guarantee that what worked for me in the current version of pfSense (v2.4.5 as of this writing) will work with future pfSense versions.

The power of pfSense lies in its configurability. However, this is also its downside until you become familiar with the product. If you don't understand what you are doing, it is possible to lock yourself out of the firewall, block your access to the internet, or cause strange network behavior. The bottom line is, **don't mess with settings other than what I describe unless you understand what you are doing**. If you find yourself in this situation, I'd suggest trying the excellent Netgate support forums for assistance and referring to the comprehensive pfSense documentation. If you do find an error in my instructions, please let me know on the support page for this book, so that I can update in future editions as appropriate.[7]

---

7. https://community.leanpub.com/c/saferhomewithpf

CHAPTER 1
THE BASIC INGREDIENTS

S o, how to get started? Step one is to purchase an SG-1100 appliance[1] or build your firewall using the pfSense community edition software.[2]

Once you have your SG-1100 in hand, follow the initial startup instructions at https://docs.netgate.com/pfsense/en/latest/ solutions/sg-1100/ to get your pfSense box set up and connected to the Internet. One change I have made to these instructions that you will see reflected later in this book is that I use 192.168.10.0/24 as the LAN subnet instead of the default 192.168.1.0/24. The reason for this is some Internet of Things (IoT) devices will use the 192.168.1.x subnet as their default as well. Plugging them into an existing 192.168.1 subnet can potentially cause conflicts with addressing. By changing the pfSense

---

1. https://shop.netgate.com/products/1100-pfsense
2. https://www.pfsense.org/download/

default LAN subnet, you can avoid addressing issues down the road.

After you have finished the initial configuration for your SG-1100, you need to set up the DHCP server for your LAN so that new devices will be assigned a dynamic IP address as they connect. To do so, go to **Services / DHCP Server / LAN** and:

- Check the **Enable** checkbox.
- For range, set an appropriate span for the IPs you will assign. Assuming you have created your LAN subnet as 192.168.10.0/24, I recommend setting your DHCP range from 192.168.10.100 to 192.168.10.199. Using this range will make it easier to differentiate DHCP-assigned addresses from static IP addresses you may assign later.
- Confirm your page looks like Figure 1 and click the blue **Save** button.

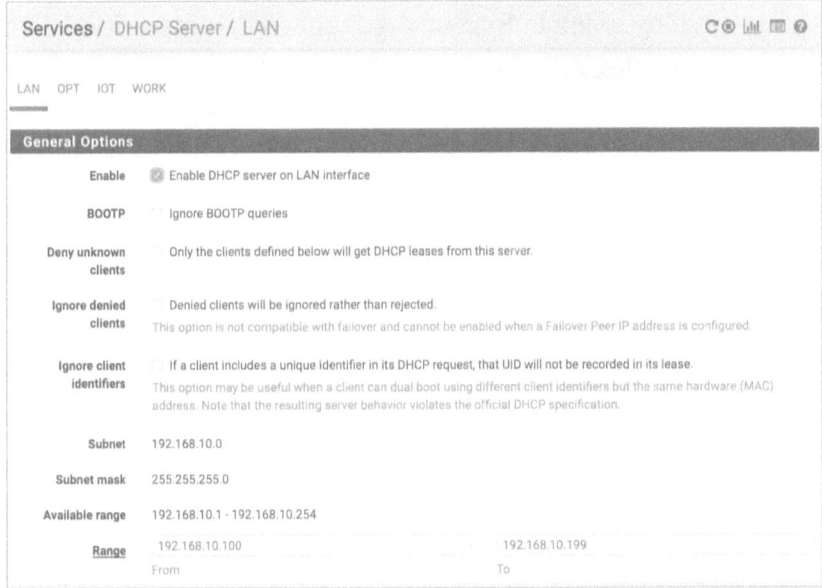

Figure 1: General Options

When you are done with the basic setup, here are a few additional tweaks I recommend:

- Uncheck the **Override DNS** checkbox when setting the Primary and Secondary DNS servers as described in the initial configuration instructions. This change will ensure that the Google DNS servers specified in the setup instructions (8.8.8.8 and 8.8.4.4) will be used regardless of the DNS servers your ISP tries to force you to use. You will have a chance to customize this in a later recipe.
- Unless you need to use IPv6, I recommend disabling it so that devices on your network cannot use IPv6 to bypass your firewall's defenses. All recipes in this book assume IPv4 addresses only. You can disable

3

IPv6 by going to **System / Advanced / Networking** and unchecking the box **Allow IPv6**.

- Set up your firewall to alert you when needed. Go to **System / Advanced / Notifications** and enter an email address for alerting. I recommend creating a new Gmail account specifically for alerting so that you can make Gmail rules as needed to process these alerts and so that any alert messages do not get lost in all your other emails. Be sure to click the **Test SMTP Settings** button to ensure your email settings are correct.

After you have completed the instructions above, you should now have the following configured on your SG-1100:

- Your local network subnet is defined.
- You have changed the admin password.
- Your DHCP server is set up.
- Your time zone is set correctly.
- You have connected your SG-1100 to your cable modem or whatever device provides your internet connection.

Finally, change your PC's IP settings back to DHCP from manual, as described in the setup instructions, and restart your PC to be assigned a new dynamic IP address in the range you defined above.

You can now test that everything is working by browsing the Internet from a computer connected to the SG-1100's LAN port (or a computer connected to a switch connected to the SG-1100's LAN port).

You're all set! You can add any or all of the remaining recipes in this book to suit your needs. Enjoy!

CHAPTER 2
ADDING PACKAGES

To use many of the recipes I will describe further in this book, you will need to install some additional software packages on your SG-1100. Don't worry; there is no cost to install them, and having them available is one of pfSense's best features, as they allow you to extend the functionality of the pfSense software based on your needs.

To install a package, log into your SG-1100 and then go to **System / Package Manager**. Once on the package manager page, select Available Packages and wait for it to populate. Your screen should look like Figure 2.

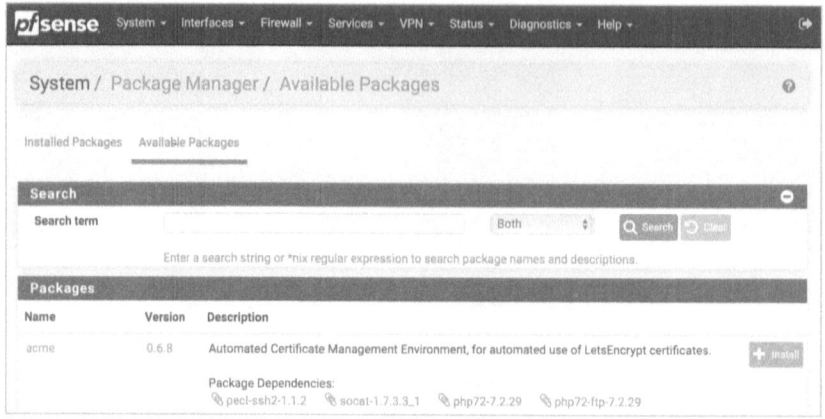

Figure 2: Available Packages

The three packages you will want to add to support the recipes later in this book are:

- pfBlockerNG-devel
- mailreport
- arpwatch

To install a package, click the green **Install** button next to the package you wish to install. You will then install each package one at a time. Be sure to stay on the package installation page while it is installing—going to another page in the middle of installing can cause the installation to fail.

DO NOT install any other packages at this time, regardless of how tempting they may seem. The SG-1100 has limited memory and cannot support running all the packages available. In particular, I do not recommend running the packages Snort or Suricata on the SG-1100.

My reasons for this are: 1) because I don't think that the SG-1100 has enough horsepower to run these well, and 2) because I believe the whole IDS/IPS paradigm is obsolete with so much traffic being encrypted these days. The DNS firewall solutions that I recommend in this book are I believe both faster and more effective at detecting and blocking malicious traffic than signature-based packet inspection, which is how Snort/Suricata operates.

CHAPTER 3
BLOCK MALICIOUS DOMAINS

B locking access to porn, phishing, and other malicious websites for all the devices on your home network is easy to do when you make use of the free DNS services from the DNS provider Cleanbrowsing.org. While you could set up and manage these filters using the squid and squidGuard packages from pfSense, you will get better results and performance if you let CleanBrowsing take care of it for you.

To set this up, from your pfSense webpage, go to **System / General Setup** and change the **DNS Servers** fields to the IP addresses of the CleanBrowsing Adult Filter servers (185.228.168.10 and 185.228.169.11) as shown in Figure 3.

These DNS servers will block access to all adult, pornographic and explicit sites, as well as malicious and phishing domains. They do not block proxy or VPN sites or mixed-content sites like Reddit. The Google and Bing search engines are set to Safe Mode so that searching for adult content is blocked.

Figure 3: DNS Server Settings

These DNS server IP addresses are the same whether you are protecting your DNS queries using DNS over TLS (DoT), as described in "Chapter 4 - Protect your browsing", or just using regular DNS. If you want less restrictive or more restrictive filters, the IP addresses for these free options are available on the CleanBrowsing website.[1]

To test whether these filters are working correctly, try browsing to a known adult website such as playboy.com. If you have set up pfSense correctly, you will receive a message similar to Figure 4, depending on your browser.

Safari Can't Open the Page

Safari can't open the page "https://www.playboy.com" because Safari can't establish a secure connection to the server "www.playboy.com".

Figure 4: Confirming Filtering Working

Likewise, you can test that SafeSearch is enforced for search engines by googling for the term "porn." Instead of returning

---

1. https://cleanbrowsing.org/filters

links to porn sites, the results page will filter these and show that SafeSearch is on, as shown in Figure 5.

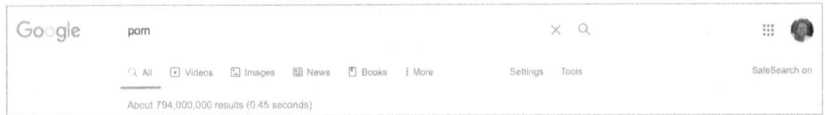

Figure 5: Verifying Safe Search

CHAPTER 4
PROTECT YOUR BROWSING

Most people are not aware that many Internet Service Providers (ISPs) collect information on the websites they browse. ISPs use this information for purposes ranging from profiling users for targeted advertising to monitoring them for potential copyright infringement.

Take back your privacy! With the enhancements made in the DNS protocols over recent years, it is now possible to hide your internet browsing from your ISP. If you switched to the Clean-Browsing DNS services as I recommended in "Chapter 3 - Block malicious domains", you can enhance that service even further by using their DNS over TLS option to shield your browsing habits from your ISP.

When you send a regular DNS request to an ISP or a 3rd party DNS provider, that request is unencrypted, which means anyone in the middle can see (and log) what website you are browsing. When you switch to DNS over TLS, that request is encrypted so only the DNS service provider can see the website for which you requested the IP address. And, if you use a DNS service provider like CleanBrowsing, which does not keep logs for their free services, you have one less privacy concern to deal with.

Start by going to **Services / DNS Resolver** to enable this on your firewall. Once there:

- Confirm that the **Enable** checkbox is checked.
- Check the **Enable SSL/TLS Service** checkbox.
- For **Network Interfaces**, select all interfaces in the dropdown except "All" and "WAN".
- For **Outgoing Network Interfaces**, select "WAN".
- Check the **DNSSEC** checkbox.
- Check both **DNS Query Forwarding** checkboxes.
- Click the blue **Save** button at the bottom of the screen.

Note that you cannot make these changes with just any DNS provider — the provider must support DNS over TLS and DNSSEC. CleanBrowsing supports both, and even better, they do so with the same IP address for the free filter you have chosen in "Chapter 3 - Block malicious domains". pfSense will make the appropriate port changes for you when you enable this option, so there is nothing else you need to change on this page. If you are not using CleanBrowsing as your DNS provider, you will need to make sure that you adjust the IP addresses on the **System / General Setup** page to the correct IP address for DNS over TLS support for the DNS provider you have chosen.

Congratulations! Your DNS requests are now shielded from your ISP's potentially prying eyes.

CHAPTER 5
BLOCK ADVERTISING

Advertising on websites has grown to be such a problem that for popular websites, it can now take longer to render the ads on a webpage than it does to show the content you care about. But hope is not lost; the pfBlockerNG plugin you enabled in "Chapter 2 - Adding packages" can be used to cut down on the burden of advertising dramatically.

This capability, called DNSBL (for DNS Block List) in the pfBlockerNG package, makes it easy to add lists of advertising and tracking servers that your firewall will automatically update and maintain, and use for blocking connections to these websites.

To start, go to **Firewall / pfBlockerNG**. Ensure the **Enable** button is checked, and click the red **Feeds** link near the top of the page. Scroll down to **DNSBL Category** and click the + button next to **EasyPrivacy** and **EasyList Adware Filter**. The + will change to a checkmark, as shown in Figure 6.

Figure 6: DNSBL Category

Now, scroll further and click the + button next to **ADs Adaway**. This will enable all the feeds in that group, as shown in Figure 7.

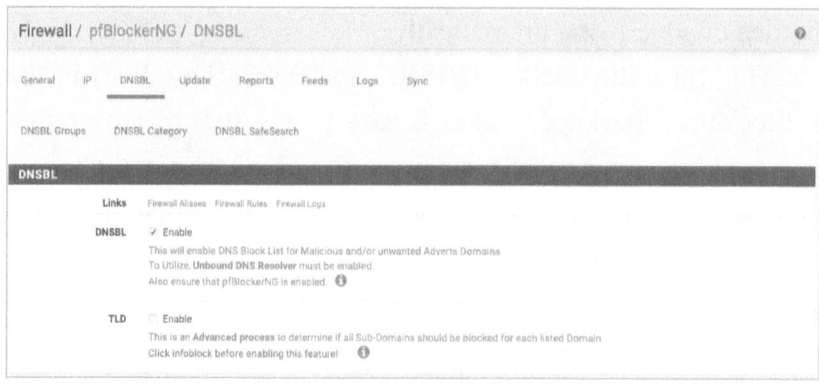

Figure 7: DNSBL Ads

Next, click the red **DNSBL** link at the top of the page. As shown in Figure 8, make sure that the **DNSBL Enable** checkbox is checked on this page.

Figure 8: DNSBL Settings

Finally, click the **DNSBL Groups** link under **DNSBL** and for the EasyList and ADs groups shown:

- Set **Action** to "Unbound".
- Set **Frequency** to "Once a Day".
- Set **Logging** to "Enabled'.
- Your webpage should match Figure 9.

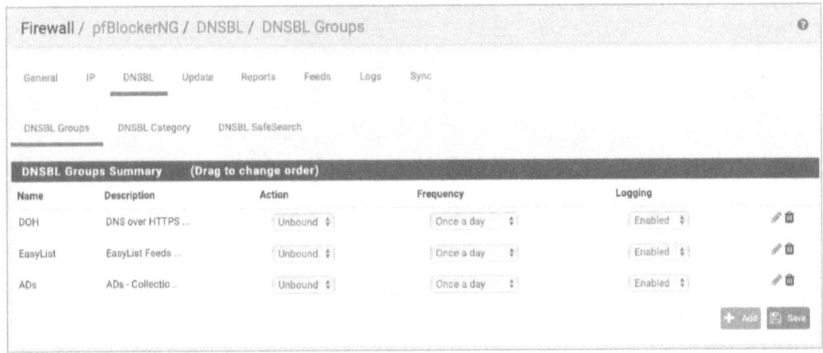

Figure 9: DNSBL Groups

Note that after making these changes, it can take up to an hour before they are applied automatically by pfSense. You can force an immediate update by clicking on the red **Update** link, and then, as shown in Figure 10:

- Set **Select 'Force' option** to "Reload".
- Click the blue **Run** button.

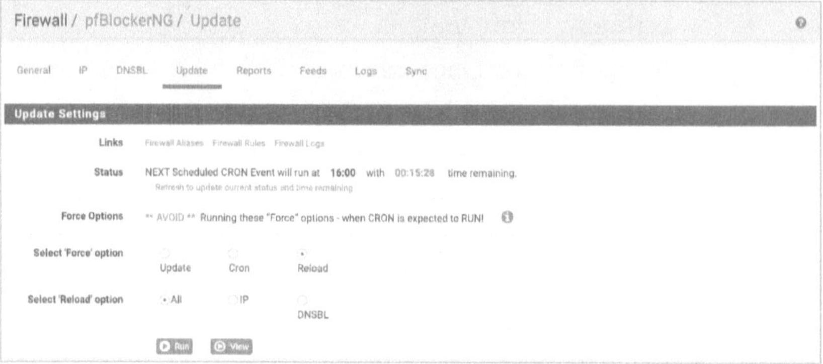

Figure 10: pfBlockerNG Update Settings

This will force an immediate update of your changes rather than waiting up to an hour for them to reload as part of the hourly refresh.

You should immediately notice a significant decrease in the number of ads on websites and an increase in page loading speed. Please note that these filters will not eliminate all ads. There is always a balance to be struck between removing more ads and causing web pages to break and not render correctly.

CHAPTER 6
CHECKING YOUR DEFENSES

S o, how can you be sure that your firewall is working correctly? One way is to look at it from the internet's (or an attacker's) perspective.

Steve Gibson from Gibson Research Corporation has created many great tools over the years, many of them free. One that I have consistently used is his Shields Up! port scanner.

This scanner will probe your firewall for open file-sharing ports, common ports, or all service ports and check to make sure UPnP is not enabled on your firewall (this is a bad thing to do). To use the scanner, go to https://www.grc.com and select the Shields Up! Test from the services menu.

To use the scanner, you only need to click **All Service Ports** under the blue ShieldsUp!! Services in the middle of the page. This tool will scan your firewall to see if you have any of the first 1056 ports (the common service ports) are open. Make sure you are on your home network behind your pfSense firewall when you run this test; otherwise, you will end up scanning someone else's firewall and not your own. What you want to see as a result is shown in Figure 11.

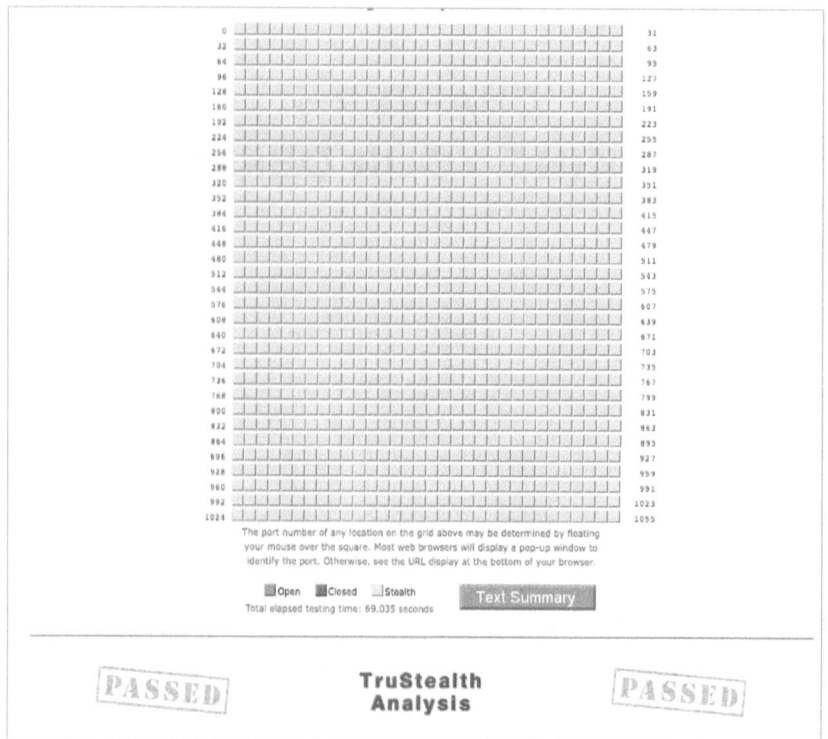

Figure 11 : ShieldsUp Output

This result confirms that your firewall has no common service ports exposed to the internet that attackers will attempt to exploit. Do this behind a typical consumer router/WiFi access point and you are likely to have very different results.

After you run this test, as a final check, run Steve's **GRC's Instant UPnP Exposure Test** on the same page. Just click the big orange button, and it will test to ensure you do not have any UPnP SSDP service running and exposed to the internet (which pfSense will not do in any case, but hey, it does not hurt to check).

As I explained above and as Steve details on his website[1], UPnP is a terrible idea. It allows any piece of consumer-grade electronics junk to open ports on your firewall for its purposes. Considering the poor security practices of most consumer electronics companies, you might as well leave your doors unlocked and windows open while you are at it.

---

1. https://www.grc.com/su/UPnP-Rejected.htm

CHAPTER 7
CORRAL THE KIDS

I n "Chapter 4 - Protect your browsing", I described how to protect one aspect of your privacy by encrypting your DNS traffic using DNS over TLS. Well, with every security enhancement it seems that we get a new security problem. In this case, the latest problem is the recent additional "enhancement" to DNS protocols called DNS over HTTPS (DoH). The fact that this is Homer Simpson's catch-phrase would not seem to be a coincidence.

DoH also encrypts DNS requests; however, instead of encrypting that traffic using TLS over port 853, it encrypts it using HTTPS over port 443. Why is that bad? Because it is now difficult for practically all network security devices (other than pfSense as I will show below) to isolate what is encrypted DNS traffic over HTTPS vs. encrypted web browsing over HTTPS. Even more of an issue is that support for this protocol is being added as an additional "feature" to major browsers such as Chrome and Firefox.

Again, you may ask, why is this bad? Because imagine this scenario; you have just implemented pfSense with "Chapter 3 - Block malicious domains" and "Chapter 4 - Protect your browsing" and are now confident that little Susie or Johnny will not be exposed to porn or other malicious websites. However, little Johnny is a stinker, and has downloaded the latest version of the Chrome browser to use DNS over HTTPS instead of the DNS setting supplied by the network or security administrator (in this case, you!).

This also applies if you have implemented pfSense to protect your small business and employees from malicious or unwanted traffic. Little Johnny (or Big Al down by the loading dock), using Chrome and its DoH capabilities, can now browse to any website they wish, circumventing any DNS-based traffic restrictions you may have in place, and you will have no idea they are doing so. This is why this is such a bad idea.

However, by leveraging the DNS blocklist capability of pfSense that you implemented in "Chapter 5 - Block advertising", you can add blocklists that will provide you at least some protection against this scourge. Using pfBlockerNG's capabilities, your firewall will use a list of domains available with pfBlockerNG to block access to these DNS DoH servers.

To add and enable this blocklist (assuming you have enabled pfBlockerNG as part of "Chapter 5 - Block advertising"), go to **Firewall / pfBlockerNG / Feeds** and then scroll down until you come to a DNSBL group called DoH. Click the blue + button to add all these feeds as a new blocklist. For the next page that shows up, set it as follows:

- Under DNSBL Source Definitions heading:
- Set the **State** next to each list to "On".

- Under the Settings heading:
- Set **Action** to "Unbound".
- Set **Update Frequency** to "Once a Day".
- Your page should look like Figure 12
- Click the blue **Save** button at the bottom of the page.

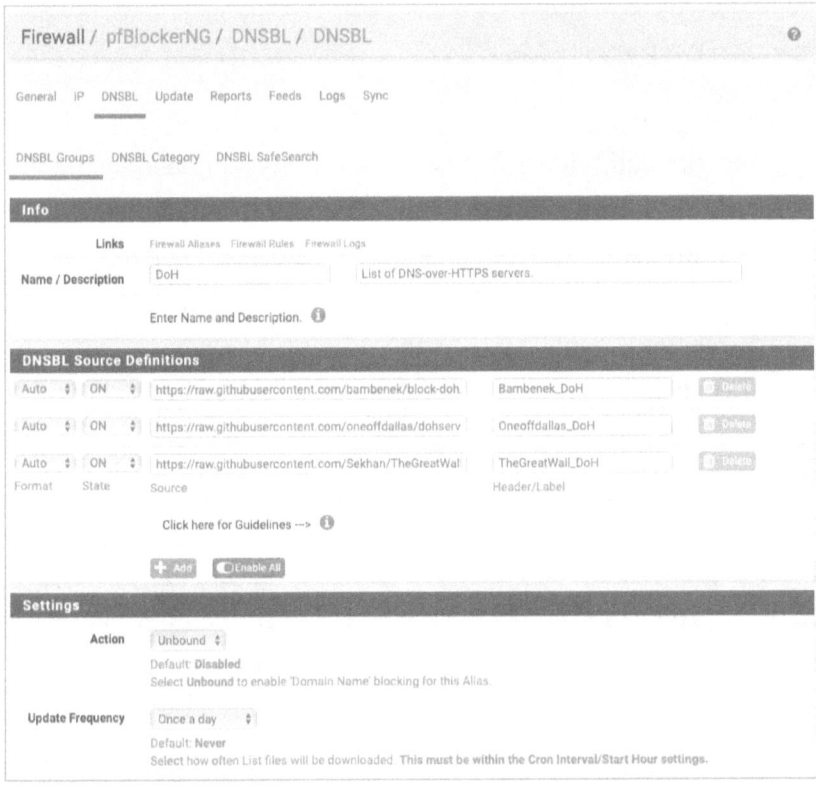

Figure 12: DNSBL

You should see the following summary page of the blocklists you have enabled, as shown in Figure 13.

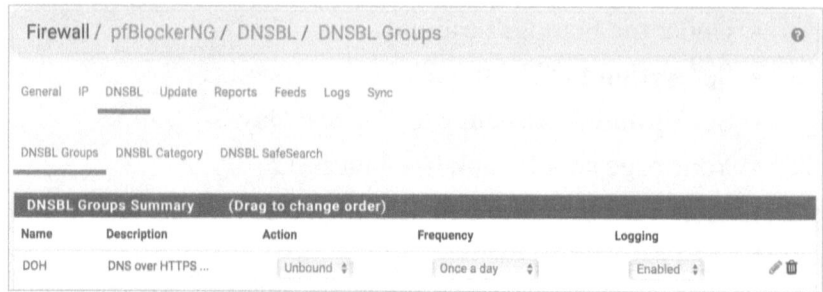

Figure 13: DNSBL Groups

Your firewall will update these blocklists daily and, using the DoH server domains listed in the blocklists, will block access attempts to these servers. If someone on your network using Firefox or some other DoH-enabled browser attempts to bypass your protections, you will see them being blocked by going to the pfBlockerNG panel on your pfSense dashboard, as shown in Figure 14. If there were a number greater than 0 showing for DNSBL_DOH, you could click that number, which will take you to a page with the details on the IP address of the sender so that you can go have a talk with whoever is attempting to bypass your controls. You can also use the methods I describe in "Chapter 14 - Monitoring your network" to create a report on this activity and have it emailed to you daily.

pfBlockerNG					🔧 ➖ ✖

MaxMind: Last-Modified: Tue, 05 May 2020 13:42:20 GMT

✅ IP	✖ 546	✔ 0	▼ 0	☰ 0	🗒
✅	✖	↺	% 100.00	☰ 509	
DNSBL	515,915	158,614			

Alias	Count	Packets 🗑	Updated	↓↑
pfB_Africa_v4	2,913	0	May 24 11:40:51	↑ (3)
pfB_Asia_v4	7,944	396	May 24 11:40:52	↑ (3)
pfB_Europe_v4	11,940	48	May 24 11:40:54	↑ (3)
pfB_PRI1_v4	15,909	6	May 27 09:02:13	↑ (3)
pfB_SAmerica_v4	4,567	90	May 24 11:40:55	↑ (3)
pfB_TOR_v4	9,049	6	May 27 09:02:15	↑ (3)
DNSBL_DOH	75	0	May 24 11:39:52	↑
DNSBL_EasyList	2,755	2366	May 27 00:00:51	↑
DNSBL_ADs	34,106	513549	May 27 00:00:53	↑

Figure 14: pfBlockerNG Dashboard Widget

So, are you done? I'm afraid not. There are still other ways that your internal users can attempt to evade the protections you have put in place. Your users can do so by directly changing the DNS settings on the network device or computer they are using to use whatever DNS servers they wish.

To block this, we want to redirect any DNS attempts by end users to bypass the firewall back to the firewall to resolve. To do so, go to **Firewall / NAT / Port Forward**, and click the green **Add Up Arrow** button to add a new NAT rule.

You will want to set up the rule as follows:

- Set **Interface** to "LAN".
- Set **Protocol** to "TCP/UDP".
- Set **Destination** to "LAN address" and click the **Invert Match** checkbox.
- Set **Destination port range From port** and **To port** to "DNS".
- Set **Redirect target IP** to "127.0.0.1".
- Set **Redirect target port** to "DNS".
- Add a description if you wish.
- Set **NAT reflection** to Disable
- Make sure **Filter rule association** is set to "Add associated filter rule"
- The page should look like Figure 15
- Click the blue **Save** button on the bottom of the page.
- Click the **Apply Changes** button that will appear at the top of the screen

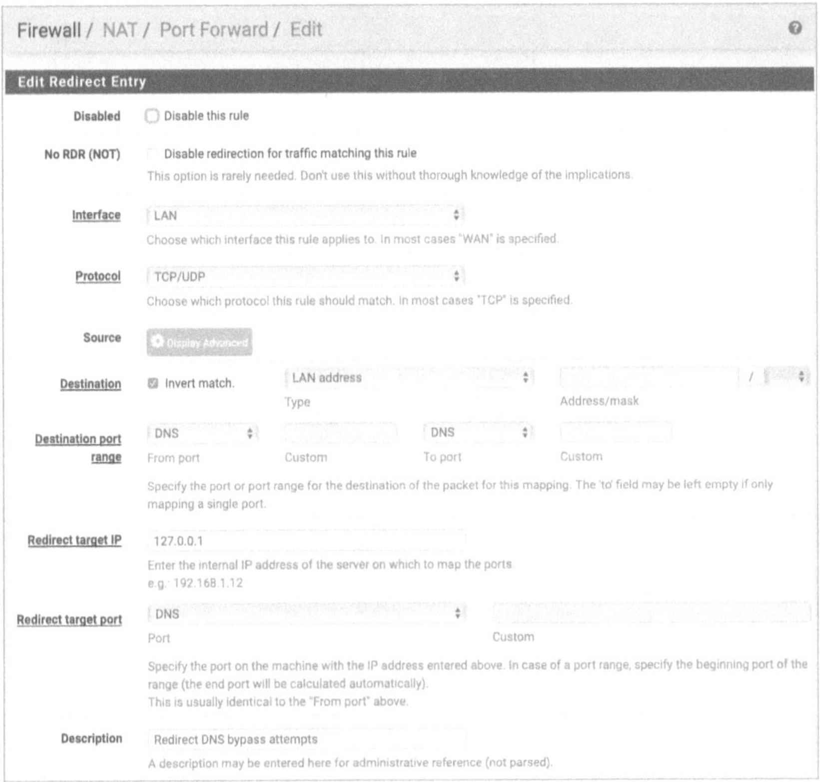

Figure 15: NAT Redirect

When you are done, return to **Firewall / Rules / LAN** and make sure your rules are ordered as shown in Figure 16. You can click and drag them to change the order. In the figure shown, I have added redirect rules for DNS over TLS (port 853) and Network Time Protocol (port 123) back to pfSense, to prevent users/apps from bypassing the firewall for these protocols.

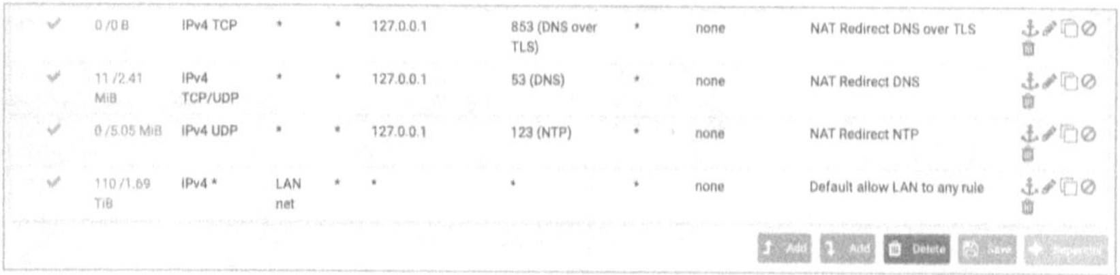

✓	0 /0 B	IPv4 TCP	*	*	127.0.0.1	853 (DNS over TLS)	*	none	NAT Redirect DNS over TLS
✓	11 /2.41 MiB	IPv4 TCP/UDP	*	*	127.0.0.1	53 (DNS)	*	none	NAT Redirect DNS
✓	0 /5.05 MiB	IPv4 UDP	*	*	127.0.0.1	123 (NTP)	*	none	NAT Redirect NTP
✓	110 /1.69 TiB	IPv4 *	LAN net	*	*	*	*	none	Default allow LAN to any rule

Add Add Delete Save

Figure 16: Firewall Rules

CHAPTER 8
SEPARATE WORK AND HOME

W ith more people working from home, separating your home and work networks is essential. Your home network is the proverbial Wild West, where anything can and will be plugged into it.

Whether it is insecure by design IoT devices or home computers infected with God-knows-what malware, keeping your work network separated from your home network will help protect your work PC from being infected by these threats and subsequently infecting your company's network. Speaking from experience, it will also help your company's security leaders sleep better at night.

Fortunately, the SG-1100 has an excellent solution for this problem out of the box. Besides the LAN port, an OPT (optional) port on the SG-1100 can be provisioned as a separate network. Rather than getting into the technicalities of provisioning a virtual LAN, which I will go over in "Chapter 9 - Isolate your

IoT", this is a quick, fast and secure way to set up a separate network for your work PC and devices.

To start, go to Interfaces / OPT and then:

- Check the **Enable** checkbox.
- Set **IPv4 Configuration Type** to "Static IPv4".
- Set **IPv4 Address** to the gateway address for the OPT interface. If you set the LAN range to 192.168.10.0/24, as I recommended in "Chapter 1 - The basic ingredients", I would suggest using 192.168.20.0/24 for the OPT subnet, in which case you want to enter "192.168.20.1" in this field.
- Set subnet mask (the field to the right of the "/") to "24".
- Confirm your settings match Figure 17.
- Click the blue **Save** button at the bottom of the page.

Figure 17: Interface Configuration

Next, go to **Services / DHCP Server / Opt** and then:

- Check the **Enable** checkbox.
- Set **Range** to whatever range you want to use for providing DHCP addresses on the OPT interface. You don't need a broad range since you will likely only have one device plugged into the interface. I'd suggest something like "192.168.20.2" to "192.168.20.10".
- Click the blue **Save** button at the bottom of the page.

Next, go to **Firewall / Rules / OPT**, and click the green **Add** button with the up arrow. On the page that appears, enter:

- Set **Protocol** to "Any" from the dropdown.
- Set **Destination** to "LAN Net" from the dropdown and check the **Invert Match** checkbox (this will block all traffic from the OPT network to the LAN but still allow access to the internet).
- Click the blue **Save** button at the bottom of the page.
- Click the green **Apply Changes** button that appears.

Finally, go to **Firewall / Rules / LAN** and add a rule to block access from the LAN network to the OPT network, as you did for the OPT network to the LAN network. There is already a default "allow LAN to any rule" — you want to add your blocking rule right above this, as shown in Figure 18. You can rearrange these rules by clicking and dragging them in the interface.

✕ ▦	0/0 B	IPv4 *	LAN net	*	OPT net	*	*	none	Block LAN access to OPT
✓ ▦	40 /184.93 GiB	IPv4 *	LAN net	*	*	*	*	none	Default allow LAN to any rule

Figure 18: Firewall Rules

You're done! You can now plug your work PC into the OPT interface of the SG-1100 with some assurance that it will be protected from whatever is on your home LAN network (and vice versa — your work PC won't be able to spy on your home network).

CHAPTER 9
ISOLATE YOUR IOT

This advanced recipe will describe how to configure your SG-1100, a managed switch, and a VLAN-capable WiFi access point to isolate your IoT devices from your LAN network.

Why bother, you ask? IoT devices (webcams, thermostats, toasters, outdoor grills and any other consumer device that connects to the internet) are notorious for being poorly designed (from a security perspective) and cannot usually be patched when vulnerabilities are found in them, which occurs constantly.

Rather than allowing these devices to be an attack vector to the PCs and other information storage and processing devices on your network, you should separate the two classes of devices onto their own networks. With pfSense, this is easy to do.

In "Chapter 8 - Separate work and home", you isolated your work PC from your home network to prevent it from interfering with or accessing home data, and vice versa. Now, we are going to extend that concept, but instead of using a physical interface on the SG-1100 as we did in the earlier recipe, we are going to create a virtual network (or VLAN) for our IoT devices.

Note that if you are going to implement this recipe, you will need to purchase or update other network components. In particular, you will need a managed/smart switch that supports VLANs and a WiFi access point with the same capability.

Fortunately, devices with this capability are readily available and relatively inexpensive. I will walk you through how to do this with my recommendations. You are certainly welcome to purchase other equipment as long as the devices you get have the same capabilities. Just be aware that they are different devices and will also have different methods to do what I will be reviewing—you will be on your own to figure out how to apply my instructions to these different devices.

For a smart switch, I recommend the TP-Link TL-SG108E[1] Gigabit switch. This eight-port switch is available at major retailers for only $30, an amazingly low price considering its capabilities. Other TP-Link models with more ports are available if you need more hard-wired ports.

For WiFi, you will need an access point that supports VLANs, assuming that many, if not most, IoT devices connect via WiFi and not with ethernet cables. In this case, I recommend Ubiquiti Access Points[2]. They have a wealth of models available for scenarios ranging from coverage for your home or small business through to a massive sports complex requiring hundreds of access points. A Unifi FlexHD Access Point[3] would be a good starting point for most homes. You will also need a PC (Mac or

---

1. https://www.tp-link.com/us/home-networking/8-port-switch/tl-sg108e/
2. https://store.ui.com/collections/unifi-network-wireless
3. https://store.ui.com/collections/unifi-network-wireless/products/unifi-flexhd

Windows) to set up and configure the access point using the Ubiquiti controller software; however, the PC does not need to be dedicated to this task once setup is complete.

Okay, with this set of recommendations, let's walk through the configuration process. I'll break this into three sections to cover the devices you will need to configure—first, your SG-1100, then your switch (the TL-SG108E), and finally, your Ubiquiti Access Point.

SG-1100 VLAN CONFIGURATION

Setting up VLANs on an SG-1100 differs from how you do so on other Netgate models or if you have a home-built firewall. This is because of the System on a Chip (SOC) that powers the SG-1100. This SOC uses VLANs internally to manage the three available ethernet ports. As a result, what I describe here cannot be directly translated to other pfSense firewalls — you will need to adjust depending on the hardware you are using.

First, go to **Interfaces / Assignments / VLANs**. On the page that is displayed, click the green + **Add** button, and on the page that is displayed, enter the following information:

- For **VLAN Tag**, enter "30".
- For **Description**, enter "IoT vLAN".
- Click the blue **Save** button, and you will be returned to the listing of all the VLANs, which should now look like Figure 19.

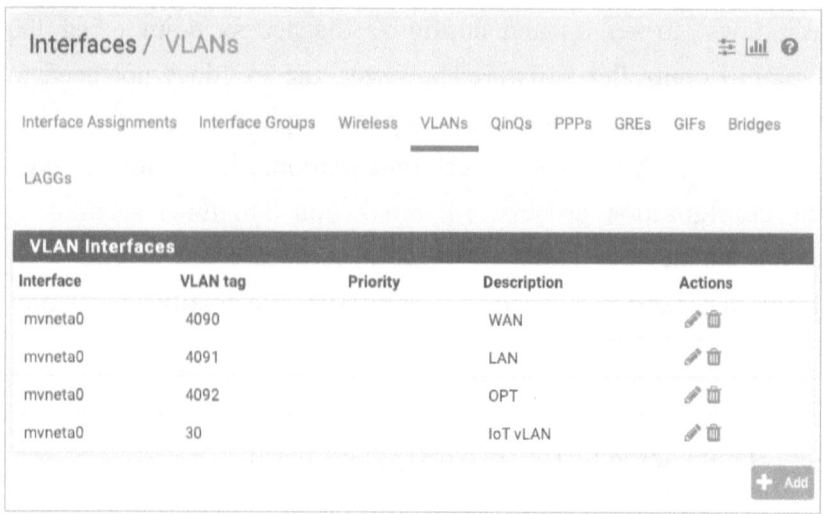

Figure 19: VLAN Table

Next, go to **Interfaces / Assignments**. Set up the VLAN subnet as follows:

- Where you see **Available network ports:**, select "VLAN 30" from the dropdown list.
- Click the green + **Add** button next to it.
- It will now show in the list as OPT2.
- Click on OPT2 so that we can rename the interface.
- On the page that appears, click the **Enable** checkbox.
- Type "IOT" in **Description**.
- For **IPv4 Configuration Type**, select "Static IPv4" from the dropdown.
- In the **Static IPv4 Configuration** section that appears below, enter "192.168.30.1" in the **IPv4 Address** field.
- Select "24" from the dropdown next to the /.
- Click the blue **Save** button at the bottom of the page.

- Click the green **Apply Changes** button that will appear at the top of the page.
- When done, go back to **Interface / Assignments**, which should now look like Figure 20.

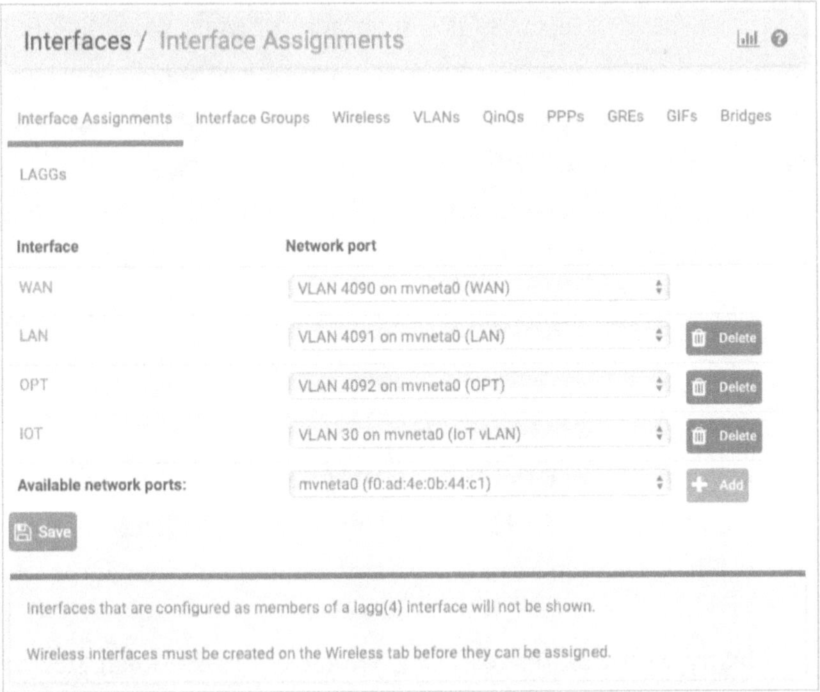

Figure 20: Interface Assignments

Next, we need to create a firewall rule for this new network. All interfaces have an implicit default deny rule at the end, so we need to add a rule to allow traffic to flow on the new subnet.

Go to **Firewall / Rules / IOT**, and click the green **Add** button with the up arrow. On the page that appears, enter:

- Set **Protocol** to "Any" from the dropdown.
- Set **Destination** to "LAN Net" from the dropdown and check the **Invert Match** checkbox (this will

block all traffic from the IoT network to the LAN but still allow access to the internet).

- Click the blue **Save** button at the bottom of the page.
- Click the green **Apply Changes** button that appears.

If you have setup the OPT interface for your work PC as I described in "Chapter 8 - Separate work and home", you will want to add another rule as described above it but, in this case, make the destination "OPT Net".

Next, we need to add a DHCP Server on the subnet, so our IoT devices will be assigned IP addresses when they connect. Go to **Services / DHCP Server / IOT**. On the page that appears:

- Check the **Enable** checkbox.
- For the **Range** fields, enter "192.168.30.100" in the left field, and "192.168.30.199" in the right field.
- Click the blue **Save** button at the bottom of the page.

Finally, as I described earlier, we have an additional step to perform because we are dealing with an SG-1100 and its SOC setup. Go to **Interfaces / Switches / VLANs**. On the page that appears, click the green **Add Tag** button, and then enter:

- For **VLAN tag**, enter 30.
- For **Description**, enter "IoT vLAN 30 on LAN Port (2)".
- For **Member(s)**, add "0" in the field.
- Click the green **Add member** button and then in the new field that appears enter "2" in the field.
- Click the blue **Save** button.

- You will be returned to the switch VLANs page, which should now look like Figure 21.

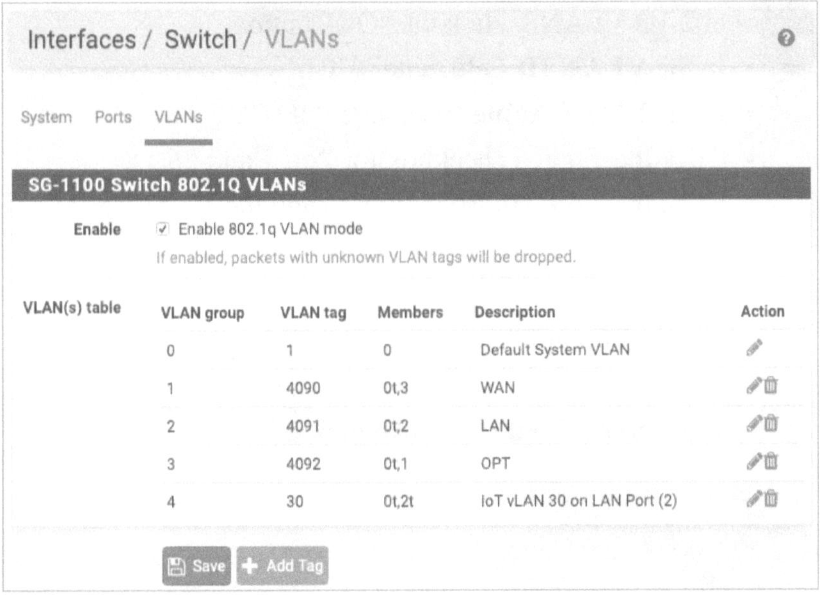

Figure 21: SG-1100 VLAN Switch

And you're done! (With the SG-1100, at least.) Next, you need to configure your smart switch, the TP-Link TL-SG108E, to properly route the VLAN traffic.

TP-LINK TL-SG108E VLAN CONFIGURATION

Assuming you have physically connected Port 1 on the TL-SG108E to the LAN port on your SG-1100, and have followed the TL-SG108E instructions to log into the device and change the default credentials, the next step is to setup your VLANs on your switch.

After logging into the TL-SG108E, go to **VLAN / 802.1Q VLAN** on the menu, and enter in the page that appears:

- For **802.1Q VLAN Configuration:**, click the **Enable** checkbox and then click the **Apply** button.
- You will be asked to confirm that you want to enable 802.1Q VLANS, click the "OK" button.
- In the **VLAN ID** field, enter "30".
- In the **VLAN Name** field, enter "IOT".
- Click the Tagged checkbox for Port 1 and Port 8.
- Click the **Add/Modify** button to add the VLAN to the switch.
- You should see an "Operation successful" banner appear for a moment at the top of the page.
- If you now enter "30" again into the **VLAN ID** field, your screen should look like Figure 22.

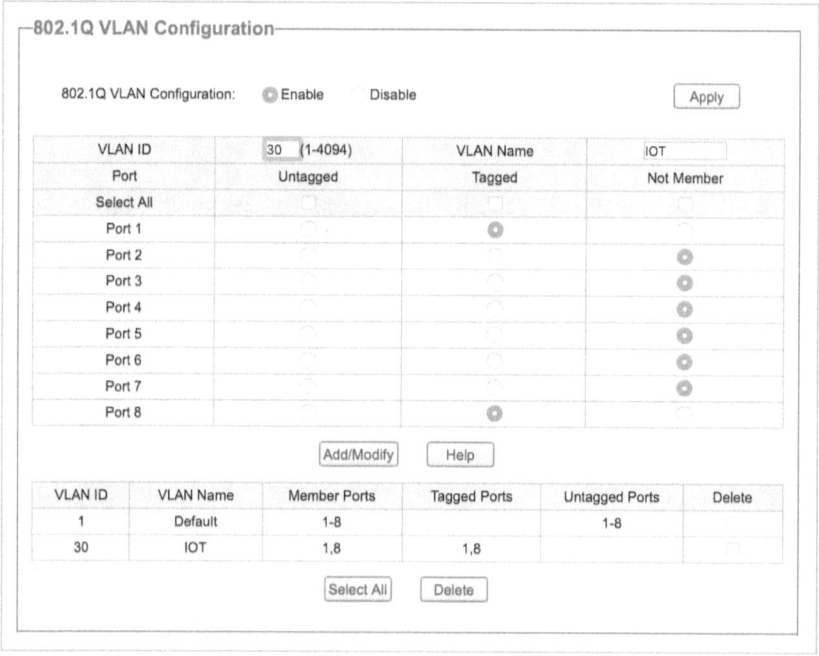

Figure 22: VLAN Configuration

And you're done with this step! You will need to connect the Unifi Access Point you purchased to Port 8 on the TL-SG108E switch (if your Unifi access point requires a POE injector for power, please be sure to use this - check the device manual for instructions). The other open ports on the switch can be used to connect any of your local devices to the LAN subnet.

UNIFI FLEXHD ACCESS POINT CONFIGURATION

And now for the final step. Connect the Unifi FlexHD Access Point to the TL-SG108E switch by using an ethernet cable from Port 8 of the switch to the POE injector that came with the access point.

Next, download the Unifi Network Controller software[4] from the Ubiquiti website that is appropriate for the type of PC you are using, and install it per the instructions for your device. After installation, adopt the access point using the Unifi controller software (See the Unifi documentation if you are unclear on how to adopt the access point).

Once you have adopted the access point and can see it in the controller software, click the Settings icon on the bottom of the left menu (it will be a gear icon).

From the settings page, select Wireless Networks. From the Wireless Networks page, click the **CREATE NEW WIRELESS NETWORK** button. On the page that appears, enter:

- For **Name/SSID**, whatever you want to use for your

---

4. https://www.ui.com/download-software/

IoT WiFi network. For this example, enter "MyIOTWiFi".

- Check the **Enabled** checkbox.
- For **Security**, select "WPA Personal".
- Enter a long, complex random password in **Security Key** (and be sure to save it).
- Click **Advanced Options** and the advanced option fields will appear.
- For **VLAN**, check the **Use VLAN** checkbox and enter "30" in the field.
- Click the green **Save** button.

Next, repeat the above instructions for your non-IOT WiFi network, naming it "MyWiFi", and skip the Advanced Options setting. When you are done, your screen should look like Figure 23.

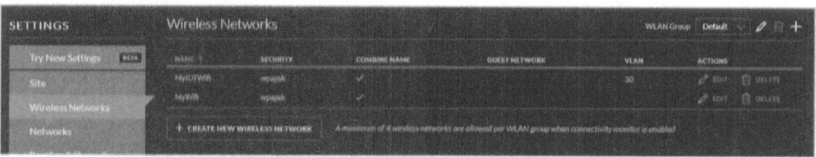

Figure 23: Unifi Settings

And you're done! You can now connect your IoT devices to the "MyIOTWiFi" network and your non-IOT devices (your PCs, etc.) to your "MyWiFi" network without concern that the poor security of your IoT devices may lead to compromise of your main computing (or work) networks.

CHAPTER 10
FIX YOUR BUFFER BLOAT

This recipe will describe how to configure your firewall to get the maximum performance from your internet connection.

Most people have probably never heard of buffer bloat. Still, it is a problem that has only become worse as high-speed internet has become more available, and more people are taking advantage of that bandwidth to stream video and other entertainment, often simultaneously on the same network.

The problem arises, as most home network problems do, from the lousy software and inadequate resources that go into most consumer-grade routers. They are simply incapable of managing the multiple competing devices on home networks today that want access to the Internet, and the result is everything from frozen video streaming to broken and terrible VOIP connections to jerky and frozen internet browsing.

TEST YOUR SPEED

Before you begin implementing the fix for buffer bloat, it's best to start by seeing if it is the cause of your problems. You can do so by using the free buffer bloat test on the DSL Reports website[1].

Just click the button on the DSL Reports page for your internet connection type (cable, DSL, etc.), and the test will run automatically. On the results page, you are looking for an "A" or "A+" in the BufferBloat circle that will appear when the test completes. If you have anything less than a "A" grade, I would suggest implementing the fixes I will describe next.

FIX YOUR BLOAT

To fix your buffer bloat problem, go to **Firewall / Traffic Shaper / Limiters and** click the green **New Limiter** button.

On the page that appears:

- Check the **Enable** checkbox.
- In the **Name** field, give the limiter a name. Since we are starting with your download limiter first, let's call it "WAN_Down."
- For **Bandwidth**, take 95% of the download speed reported when you tested your internet connection. So, if DSL Reports reported your WAN download speed as 100 Mbs, then set Bandwidth to 95 Mbs. One note of warning, if DSL Reports is showing a speed higher than what you know you have purchased

---

1. https://www.dslreports.com/speedtest

from your provider, use your provider's speed as the max. For example, if you have a 100 Mbs down service from your cable provider but DSL Reports shows 120 Mbs in the test, use 100 Mbs as the maximum and take 95% of that. The higher speeds you see are generally transient; if you use them in most cases, this fix will not work properly.

- Set **Queue Management Algorithm** to "CoDel".
- Set **Scheduler** to "FQ_CODEL".
- Set the **Queue length** to "1000".
- Check the **ECN** checkbox for Explicit Congestion Notification.
- Click the blue **Save** button at the bottom of the page.
- Click the **Apply Changes** button at the top of the page.

Next, you need to add a queue to the limiter you just created. On the same page, click the green **+ Add new Queue** button at the bottom of the page. On the page that appears:

- Check the **Enable** checkbox.
- Give the queue a name. In this case, I would suggest "WAN_Down_Queue" in the **Name** field.
- Set **Queue Management Algorithm** to "CoDel".
- Check the **ECN** checkbox for Explicit Congestion Notification.
- Click the blue **Save** button at the bottom of the page.
- Check the **Apply Changes** button at the top of the page.

Now, you must repeat these steps for your upload limiter and queue. Create a new limiter, except call it "WAN_Up" with the bandwidth set to 95% of what you observed with DSL Reports for upload speed. After you do that, create a queue under it named "WAN_Up_Queue". Repeat all the setting selections you made for the down limiter and queue.

Now, you must create a firewall rule to apply these limiters to traffic on your WAN interface. Go to **Firewall / Rules / Floating**, and click the green **Add** button with the up arrow.

On the page that comes up (**Firewall / Rules / Floating / Edit**):

- Check the **Quick** checkbox.
- Set **Interface** to "WAN".
- Set **Direction** to "out".
- Set **Address Family** to "IPv4".
- Set **Protocol** to "Any".
- Click the blue **Advanced** button.
- In the advanced options that appear, scroll down to **Gateway** and select your gateway from the options. There should only be your gateway or "Default" as options. Do not leave it as "Default".
- Next for **In / Out pipe**, for **In** (the left dropdown), select "WAN_Up_Queue".
- For **Out** (the right dropdown), select "WAN_Down_Queue".
- Click the blue **Save** button at the bottom of the page.
- Check the **Apply Changes** button at the top of the page.

You're done! Go back to DSL Reports and run the test again.

If you have done everything correctly, you should now see A or A+ in the BufferBloat button results, and you should notice significantly better performance with all the competing services that are using your internet connection.

CHAPTER 11
DIALING IN FROM THE ROAD

This recipe will describe configuring your firewall's Virtual Private Network (VPN) service to enable secure remote access from the road.

Before I describe how to do this, let me ask you, "Why"? Do you really need access back to your local network? The reason I ask is that every port you open on your firewall, and this will involve opening a port, exposes you to many more attacks and potential exploits of vulnerabilities that may exist, either in the VPN software or in the credentials you are using for the VPN.

While pfSense has an excellent record of being secure software to start and patching flaws as they are discovered, the fact remains that all software is subject to vulnerabilities. Every port that you open on your firewall, particularly ports for remote access, will be discovered and relentlessly probed and attacked by foreign and domestic attackers. I speak from experience here.

Personally, I would rather have peace of mind and know that

by not exposing such holes, I have one less thing to worry about on my firewall. But if that's what you need, here is how you go about doing it.

GETTING BACK TO YOUR FIREWALL

Step one is getting back to your firewall from the internet. Unless your connection to the internet comes with a static IP address, you are likely to be assigned a dynamic IP by your ISP. So, unless you plan on constantly checking your firewall for changes to your WAN IP address, I'd recommend using a Dynamic DNS service that links a static URL address to your dynamic WAN IP address. pfSense conveniently supports this service as a built-in capability. If you do have a static IP for your WAN connection, you can skip this step and proceed to the next section.

pfSense offers a wide variety of dynamic DNS service providers to choose from; however, I recommend a simple one that I have used in the past. To start, go to https://freemyip.com. On the website that appears, claim your domain by picking a name for your network, such as "Bobsfamilynetwork," and clicking the red **Check Availability** button. If the one you chose has already been taken, try others that are meaningful to you until you find one that is free.

When you find one that is available, you will be presented with a page saying that the domain is available. Click the red **CLAIM IT!** button.

Now, you will be presented with a page saying that the domain was added, and you will see the URL you need to use to update your IP address. SAVE THIS INFORMATION!, as it is the only way to update your dynamic IP address, and there is no way to recover it. If you forget it or leave this page without copying it, you will have to wait a year before you can try to reclaim that same network name.

Next, take the URL you copied and securely saved, and go to **Services / Dynamic DNS**. Click the green + **Add** button to add a new dynamic DNS client.

On the page that pops up next (**Services / Dynamic DNS / Dynamic DNS Clients / Edit**):

- Select "Custom" from the **Service Type** drop-down list.
- Enter the URL you copied from the FreemyIP page into the **Update URL** field.
- Click the blue **Save** button at the bottom of the page.

That's it! You will now be returned to the Dynamic DNS Clients page, where you should see your new entry. If the IP under Cached IP is green, you are good to go, as this indicates that it has been updated on the FreemyIP website. You can now refer to your local network using the URL of <My network name>.freemyip.com. Your pfSense firewall will update the IP of this URL automatically whenever the IP of the WAN interface changes.

SETTING UP OPENVPN IN PFSENSE

Once you have your DDNS name set up (assuming you don't have a static IP for your internet connection), you need to set up the VPN in pfSense itself.

Go to **System / Package Manager** and install the openvpn-client-export package. You will use this at the end of your pfSense setup.

Next, go to **VPN / OpenVPN / Wizards**. The wizard simplifies the OpenVPN setup, as you will use the default options for most settings.

The page will now show **the Wizard / OpenVPN Report Access Server setup**. For **the Type of Server**, leave it at the default "Local User Access." Click the blue **Next** button.

You will now need to create a certificate for use by your VPN. To start, enter:

- For **Descriptive name**, give the certificate a name such as "MyVPNCert".
- For **Country Code** enter "US" (or whatever your country code is).
- Fill out **State or Province**, **City**, and **Organization** as appropriate for your setup.
- Click the blue >> **Add new CA** button on the bottom of the page.

Next you will be taken to a page to add your server certificate. All the information will have been transferred from the prior page, all you need to do it give the certificate a unique name such as "MyServerCert". Click the blue >> **Create new Certificate** button at the bottom of the page.

Now for the fun part, you should be at the **Wizard / OpenVPN Remote Access Server setup / Server** setup page. Leave all the default options in place and scroll down to the Tunnel Settings section. Enter:

- For **the Tunnel Network**, choose a subnet that you are not already using, such as 192.168.100.0/24.
- Check the **Redirect Gateway** checkbox if you want to force all traffic from your remote client back through the VPN when it is enabled, otherwise leave it unchecked to allow split tunneling at the client (this will depend on your use case). Be aware that if you do check the box, ALL traffic from the client to the internet will be directed back through your firewall, which, depending on what else they are doing remotely (streaming video, for example), could be a large volume.
- Enter in **Local Network** the networks that you want the VPN user to be able to connect to. Normally, this is the LAN but could be your IoT network if you set up a separate IoT network following "Chapter 9 - Isolate your IoT". For example, for LAN, enter 192.168.10.0/24 if you have followed the IP recommendations I have made in this book.
- Set **Concurrent Connection** to however many users will use this connection. If it is just you, I suggest setting it to 1.
- Click the blue >> **Next** button at the bottom of the screen.

Now, you will be taken to a page to configure the firewall rules. Check both the **Firewall Rule** and **OpenVPN rule** checkboxes to have the wizard take care of these chores for you.

Click the blue >> **Next** button at the bottom of the page.

And you're done! The page showing should now say that the

configuration is complete. Click the blue >> **Finish** button at the bottom to exit the wizard.

SETTING UP YOUR MOBILE DEVICE TO USE YOUR VPN

Now, to take advantage of the OpenVPN server you have just created. Unfortunately, I cannot get into all the details for installing VPN certificates considering the wide variety of devices out there, but it just involves picking the configuration that matches the device your remote VPN user will be using, and installing the configuration file into the OpenVPN software on that device.

To start, you need to create remote user credentials for the person who will use the VPN connection. Go to **System / User Manager and** click the green + **Add** button.

On the page that follows, enter:

- For **Username**, give the user a name without spaces.
- For **Password**, enter and confirm a complex password.
- Check the box for **Certificate** to create a user certificate.
- For **Descriptive name**, give the certificate a name such as "MyCert". Leave the other fields in this section to their defaults.
- The **Certificate authority** should already be defaulted to the VPN certificate you created earlier.
- Click the blue **Save** button.

Now go to **VPN / OpenVPN / Client Export**. Fill in as follows:

- The **Remote Access Server** should already have the VPN server you just created already preselected.
- For **Host Name Resolution**, if you are using a static IP to get access to your server, select "Interface IP address" from the dropdown. If you have set up Dynamic DNS as described in the first section of this recipe, select "Other", and in the **Host Name** field that appears, enter the URL provided by your dynamic DNS provider.
- Click the blue **Save as default** button.
- Scrolling down to the bottom of the page, you will see VPN user you just added along with all the options you have for download VPN client installer packages as shown in Figure 24.
- Click the blue configuration button appropriate for the device your remote user is using to download the configuration file or package to your PC. Then, upload it to the OpenVPN client software for that device. Check the manual for the client OpenVPN software for specific instructions on how to load the configuration.

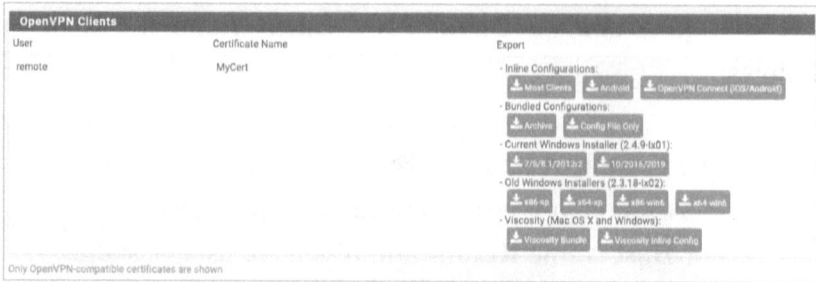

Figure 24: OpenVPN Client S/W Export

When you are done, you should now be able to use the client's remote VPN software to access your home network while on the road. Test that it is set up correctly by attempting to access a device on your IoT network that you know has a web interface, such as most network printers.

CHAPTER 12
ALERT ON NEW DEVICES

Getting alerts when new devices appear on your network is an essential part of keeping it secure. Whether it is someone who has compromised your WiFi network or someone in your business or household who has added a device you are not aware of, either event could be the precursor to a possible compromise of your network's security.

Knowing what assets you have is a vital part of any information security program, and it applies to your home network just as much as it does to businesses. Tracking new devices on your network is easy when you assign known devices a static IP address. Fortunately, pfSense makes this easy.

To start, assuming you have assigned the DHCP range for your LAN to be 100 to 199 as described in "Chapter 1 - The basic ingredients", then you will want to assign the devices in your network IPs between 2 to 99. You can also use the 200 to 254 range as well if you wish.

How you divvy up these addresses is up to you. You can do it sequentially, by device type (all webcams from 20 to 29, for example), by user (all of Timmy's devices from 30 to 39), etc. Whatever makes the most sense to you.

To set the static IP addresses, I assume that you have connected your devices to your LAN, and they have received a DHCP dynamic address in the range you have defined. Next, go to **Status / DHCP Leases**, and you will be directed to a page showing your network's dynamic and static IPs. To convert a dynamic IP to a static IP, click the hollow blue + icon next to the entry you want to convert. You will be directed to a page specific to that device, with the MAC address prefilled with the device's hardware MAC address. The fields you want to enter are:

- Add the name you want to see for the device when viewing it in pfSense logs in **Client Identifier**. Generally, I use the formula IP address, device type, and device identifier, such as "032 Roku Upstairs."
- Enter the static IP address you want the device to have in **IP address**.
- Click the blue **Save** button at the bottom of the page.

The static IP will now be defined. To force the device to take that static IP, you usually need to power it off and on. It will get the static IP you have assigned as part of its startup.

Once you have defined static IPs for all your devices and have things organized on your network the way you wish, now you need to make use of the Arpwatch package you downloaded in "Chapter 2 - Adding packages".

Go to **Services / Arpwatch**, and enter the following:

- Check the **Enable Arpwatch** checkbox.
- Under **Interfaces**, select the interface(s) you want to monitor. You can start with just LAN; you would usually not want to check WAN.
- Set the notification recipient to the email address you want to receive these alerts (assuming you set up notifications as I directed in the Introduction).
- Check all the remaining checkboxes on the page except **Disable CARP/VRRP**.
- Confirm your page matches Figure 25.
- Click the blue **Save** button at the bottom of the page.

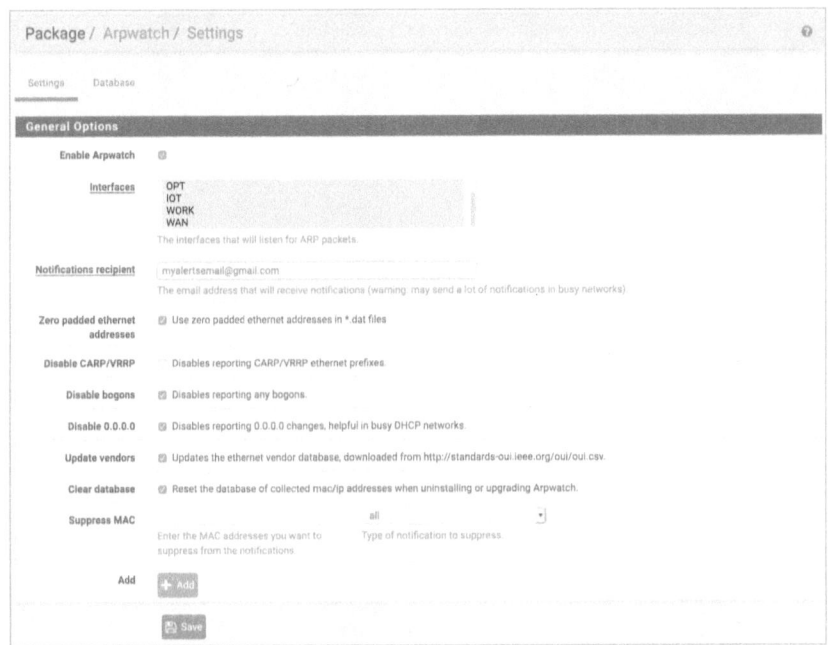

Figure 25 : Arpwatch Settings

You will now receive numerous emails, as an alert will be generated for all the devices connected to the firewall for the interfaces you are monitoring. Once you receive that initial surge of emails, you will, in the future, only receive an email when a new device shows up on a monitored interface. You will know when something new has been connected to your home network, wired or WiFi so that you can either confirm it is legitimate or investigate further if it is unknown to you.

CHAPTER 13
BLOCKING BAD ACTORS

This recipe will describe how to configure your firewall to block infected systems from inside your network from reaching out to the internet, as well as blocking access to countries that are significant sources of malware and attacks on the internet.

Studies have shown that Russia and China are the primary foreign sources of malware and attacks on the internet. Personally, when I analyzed the data on probes/attacks against my firewalls, both countries were in my top five.

So what, you might ask? I have a firewall, and its job is to block these connections. And you would be right—your pfSense will block all incoming unsolicited connection requests. But, by the same token, your firewall will not normally block any connection request originating from inside your network out to the Internet, such as when an internal system infected with ransomware reaches out to its command and control (C&C) server.

Here is where you can leverage the DNS blocking capabilities of pfBlockerNG that you installed in "Chapter 2 - Adding packages" and "Chapter 5 - Block advertising", to block compromised devices you may have inside your network from connecting to their C&C servers and downloading yet more malware to your network.

By using the capabilities of pfBlockerNG, you can identify internal connection attempts to known bad IPs, bad domains, and potentially dangerous countries such as Russia and China, where many of these domains are hosted. Let's take these one by one.

BLOCKING BAD IPS

pfBlockNG includes many lists (called feeds) of malicious IPs and domains as part of the package. These feeds are sourced from various security-focused organizations and groups that scour the internet for this information.

I recommend implementing the priority one IP blocklists, as I will describe next. As you gain experience with pfBlockerNG, you can experiment with adding additional lists; however, be aware that the more IP blocklists you implement, the higher the chances you will end up blocking legitimate IPs and causing problems with the devices on your network.

To get started, go to **Firewall / pfBlockerNG / Feeds**. At the top of the Feeds list shown, directly under the headings, you will see **IPv4 Category, Alias/Group PRI1**. There will be a blue + on the line. Click that, and it will add all the feeds in the PRI1 group to pfBlockerNG.

After clicking +, you will be directed to a page where you can confirm the feeds you are about to add. For the PRI1 list, you first want to delete the Pulsedive feed from the group by clicking the yellow **Delete** button to the right of that feed. Pulsedive requires an expensive paid subscription that I don't believe most personal users or SMBs need.

Once you have deleted this feed (it will disappear from the list of feeds), click the blue **Enable All** button under the list of feeds. The state for all the feeds will change to "ON". Next, under Settings, change **Action** from "Disabled" to "Deny Outbound". Leave all the other settings the same, and then click the blue **Save IPv4 Settings** button at the bottom of the page. After you do, you will see a message toward the top of your page that the settings have been saved, as shown in Figure 26.

Figure 26: pfBlockerNG

What will now happen is that all the feeds in the PRI1 group will update automatically every hour with the latest lists of bad IP addresses, and your firewall will block and log access to these IPs from any device inside your network.

I would next recommend repeating the process described above but for the TOR list of feeds. The reason I recommend blocking TOR (which stands for The Onion Router, a protocol and network for anonymous browsing on the Internet) is that malware has been discovered that takes advantage of this anonymity network to hide its connections back to its Command and Control (C&C) server. Unless you need to use TOR for anonymous browsing, I recommend blocking it.

When you are done, go to **Firewall / pfBlockerNG / IP / IPv4**, and you will see both feeds enabled, as shown in Figure 27.

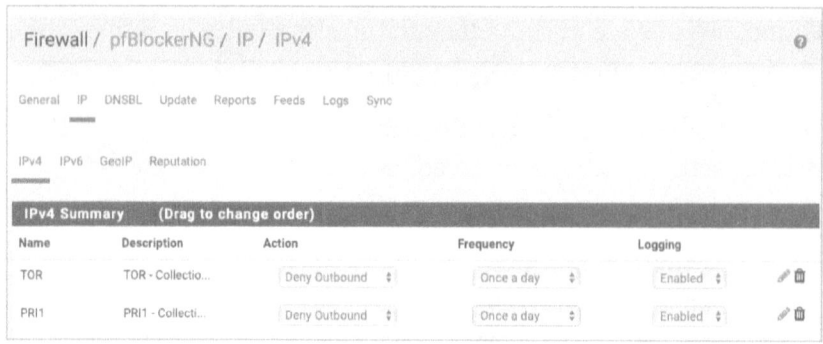

Figure 27 : pfBlockerNG Summary

Note that changes to your configurations, such as adding new feeds, will occur as part of the daily update on your pfSense firewall. If you want to force an immediate update, go to **Firewall / pfBlockerNG / Update**, and then select **Reload** next to **Select 'Force' option** and press the blue **Run** button. Doing this will force an immediate reload and update of your pfBlockedNG feed options and data.

BLOCKING BAD DOMAINS

While pfBlockerNG can block domains based on various criteria and blocklists, I recommend against this (unless you are blocking advertising, as discussed in "Chapter 5 - Block advertising"). Why do I say this?

If you are using Cleanbrowsing's DNS servers, as I recommended in "Chapter 3 - Block malicious domains", they will take care of protecting you from adult sites and malicious domains better than you can achieve on your own through building a collection of blocklists using pfBlockerNG.

CleanBrowsing also draws upon various third-party sources to select websites to block. However, it is more cautious in ensuring that its sources are low in false positives (saying a site is bad when it is not). This means you are less likely to experience problems while browsing while still being protected from the vast majority of bad sites.

What if you want to block more than just adult and malicious sites? You have two options: One, you can use the other free DNS addresses CleanBrowsing provides, which are even more restrictive on adult sites. Or, if you want to be more selective in the sites you block, you can do this using pfBlockerNG's category-blocking capability.

To enable blocking by category using pfBlockerNG, go to **Firewall/ pfBlockerNG/ DNSBL/ DNSBL Category**. From there, change **Blacklist Category** to "Enable", and change **Update frequency** to "Once a day". When you do this, all the categories to choose from will appear. Select those you wish to block and then click the blue **Save** button at the bottom of the page.

BLOCKING BAD COUNTRIES

Besides blocking IPs and malicious/adult domains, I recommend blocking all access to Russia and China, as these countries host most attacks on the internet. Likewise, any malware that infects a system on your network will likely call back to Russia or China for instructions, so blocking all access to the IPs these countries use is a quick way to stop these attacks from spreading.

To do so, go to **Firewall / pfBlockerNG / IP / GeoIP**. From that page, you will see the world's geographic breakdown under GeoIP Summary. To block China, for example:

- Click the blue pencil icon next to the Asia row, and you will be taken to a page showing all the countries in Asia you can block.
- CTRL+Click to select the two China entries.
- Scroll down the page and then for **List Action**, select "Deny Both".
- For **Enable Logging**, select "Enabled".
- Finally, click the blue **Save** button at the bottom of the page.

To block all access to Russia, select "Europe" at the top of the page. You will be taken to another page listing all the countries in Europe. Again, choose both entries for Russia and set the other options as you did for China. Save the page as well.

Return to **Firewall / pfBlockerNG / IP / GeoIP** to confirm your changes. Your screen should now look like Future 28.

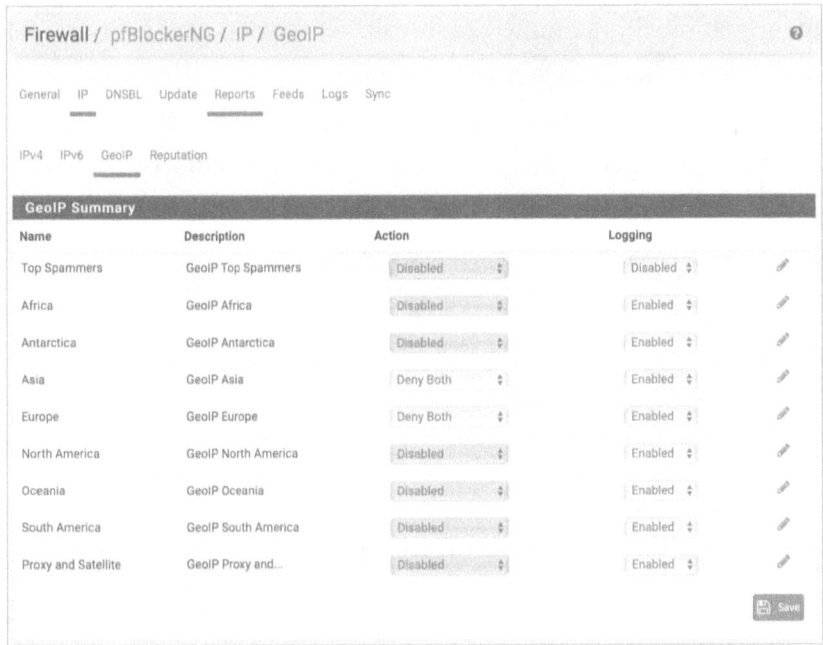

Figure 28: GeoIP Summary

FINAL WARNING

A final warning: don't expect perfection. Analysis[1] has shown that, at best, these methods can block 50-75% of internet threats. These measures should be seen as one additional layer of protection in your security stack (as I discuss in A Reality Check at the end of this book) to be combined with the software and configuration measures you (hopefully) have in place to protect your endpoint devices.

Also, don't go overboard and try to block everything. The

---

1. Baker, C. (2019, October 23). *Challenges in Effective DNS Query Monitoring.* Sans.org. https://www.sans.org/reading-room/whitepapers/dns/challenges-effective-dns-query-monitoring-39215

more you block, the more you break. At the end of the day, some protection is better than no protection.

If you impact your end users' experience, you only encourage them to circumvent these measures, which results in even less protection than when you started. The best protection measures are those that your users are unaware of.

CHAPTER 14

MONITORING YOUR NETWORK

This recipe describes how to configure your firewall to send daily reports on possible infected systems or malicious applications running inside your network.

If you followed the instructions in "Chapter 13 - Blocking bad actors", then you have successfully implemented controls to stop (some but not all) infected systems within your network from reaching out to their C&C servers. However, how will you know these systems exist on your network?

This is where you can use the log reporting feature provided by the mailreport package you installed in "Chapter 2 - Adding packages". Using this package, you will store the FreeBSD command line commands to analyze the log files as you desire. I will describe below the commands that I use myself, but as with all things Linux/BSD, these are just scratching the surface of what you can do. Consider these a starting point for your experimentation.

In my case, I want to know if any devices on my network

have triggered the rules I set up in "Chapter 13 - Blocking bad actors" to block access to malicious IPs or TOR IPs. Either could indicate that I have a device on my network that is infected with malware and thus should be investigated.

To start, go to **Status / Email Reports**, and click the green **Add New Report** button. Next, enter:

- In **Description**, enter a name for the report.
- Under the **Schedule** section, select the frequency and timing for when you want the report to run.
- Click the blue **Save** button.

Once you have saved the report, you will be taken back to the **Status / Email Reports / Edit Reports** page, listing all the reports you have created. You will receive a reminder to make sure you have your email notification settings created, as I discussed in "Chapter 1 - The basic ingredients", otherwise you would have no way to receive the reports being generated. Figure 29 shows what my list of reports looks like.

Description	Schedule	Commands	Logs	Actions
DoH Access Attempts	Daily at 01:00	1	0	✏️ 🗑️
Blocked Malicious IP Access Attempts	Daily at 01:05	2	0	✏️ 🗑️

Configure SMTP settings under System -> Advanced, on the Notifications tab

Figure 29: Email Reports

Now, click the blue pencil icon to the right of the report you just created. In this example, let's look at my Blocked Malicious IP Access Attempts report.

When you click the pencil icon, you will be taken back into the report page, however, there will now be two additional sections added, **Included Commands** and **Included Logs**. It is the **Included Commands** section that we are interested in. The **Included Logs** section allows you to send various system logs to you periodically, however outside of troubleshooting, I find that this is too much information to process daily. The **Included Commands** section allows you to store a series of commands to process and filter log data down to your interests.

I will show the entire string to enter into the Included Commands section and then break it down so you can understand what I am doing. Getting into the details of how each command works is beyond the scope of this book. The best way to learn is to enable SSH access to your pfSense firewall and play with creating these reports from the shell command line. Alternatively, you can use the command line interface from the pfSense web GUI at **Diagnostics / Command Prompt** to enter commands and test your reports.

So, here is the command to enter to have your pfSense monitor for any internal systems attempting to access malicious external IPs (again, assuming you have implemented "Chapter 13 - Blocking bad actors"):

date -v-1d '+%b %-d' | grep -f /dev/stdin /var/log/pfblock-erng/ip_block.log | grep "pfB_PRI1" | awk -F'[,]' '{ print $1, $2, $3, $11, $10, " > ", $12":"$14, "List:", $19, "URL:", $20 }'

In the Included Commands section of the page, click the green **Add New Command** button. Then enter:

- In the **Name** field, enter a name for the command. I reused the report's name.
- In the **Command** field, enter the command string I provided above.
- Click the blue **Save** button. You will be directed back to the Edit Reports page so that you can verify what you just entered, as shown in Figure 30.

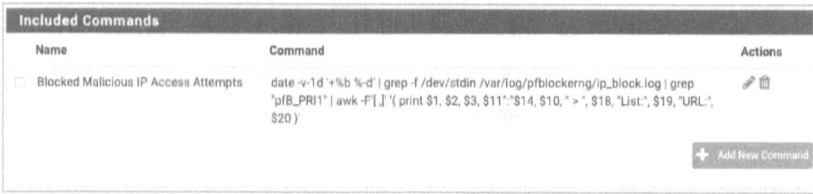

Figure 30: Included Commands

To help you better understand what this command is doing, let me break it down for you.

- First, we determine yesterday's date (assuming we are running this daily and want to find out what happened yesterday) and output this as a string.

date -v-1d '+%b %-d'

- Next, we pipe (the "|") this date string value to grep, which will be used as input to extract all the blocked log entries that occurred yesterday from the pfBlockedNG block log.

grep -f /dev/stdin /var/log/pfblockerng/ip_block.log

- Next, we pipe this subset to grep again to extract just those log entries that involve violations of the priority one blocklist we set up in "Chapter 13 - Blocking bad actors".

grep "pfB_PRI1"

- Finally, we pipe the subset of blocked log entries we are interested in to awk to make the final report more readable.

awk -F'[,]' '{ print $1, $2, $3, $11, $10, " > ", $12":"$14, "List:", $19, "URL:", $20 }'

What I have shown above is just one of a nearly infinite number of ways you can leverage BSD command-line utilities to extract and report on information from pfSense. I have used the method above to make it as readable and understandable as possible (to me, at least), but please do not think this is the only way to build your reports.

And that's it! You will now get a report daily on possibly infected systems inside your network. If there were no blocked attempts, you would get an email showing just the commands and nothing else. If there are entries, you should investigate to ensure these are not false positives and take action as needed. What action you take, from updating the device to removing it from your network, is impossible for me to say, as this depends on the device in question — you will have to use your judgment as to why the device appears in the log. Just consider anything that shows up on this report suspicious until you can justify otherwise.

Using this approach (but not the specific commands) I have described, you can generate a report on blocked access attempts to TOR, violations of firewall rules, or just about anything you wish to know about that uses information from any of the pfSense logs. The only limit is your imagination. Have fun!

CHAPTER 15
MAKING EXCEPTIONS

This recipe will describe configuring your DNS firewall (assuming you implemented pfBlockerNG in "Chapter 5 - Block advertising") to make exceptions to the rules. Sometimes, some devices dislike being blocked from snitching on you. In that case, I will show how to make exceptions for individual devices rather than turning off these protections.

My Roku devices are the perfect example of this for me. For some reason, some channels won't load or play when I have ad-blocking enabled. Rather than disable ad blocking for all the devices on a subnet, it is possible to exclude individual devices based on their IP addresses from DNSBL filtering.

To start, go to **Services / DNS Resolver / General Settings**. Then, add settings in **Custom options** at the bottom of the page to exclude the devices from DNSBL scanning.

Assuming your LAN subnet is 192.168.10.0/24, and the device you want to exclude from ad blocking is 192.168.10.14, here is what you would want to see in the **Custom options** box:

server:
access-control-view: 192.168.10.14/32 bypass
access-control-view: 192.168.10.0/24 dnsbl
view:
name: "bypass"
view-first: yes
view:
name: "dnsbl"
view-first: yes
include: /var/unbound/pfb_dnsbl.*conf

If there are multiple devices you want to exclude, just add their IPs under "server:" with a "/32" on the end. You must add each device as its own entry — one per line.

One warning, whenever you update DNSBL to a new version, you will need to likely go back in and re-add these custom options, which means that it is a good idea to keep the current configuration in your firewall journal as I describe in "Chapter 16 - Keeping good records".

Also, the order of these settings matter. They need to be added exactly as shown. A common problem that has happened to me is that the custom options will reset to "server include: /var/unbound/pfb_dnsbl.*conf" when pfBlockerNG is updated. If this is not corrected when the custom options you saved in your journal are readded, it will invalidate everything above it.

Again, set it up as shown in the example above. The best way to be sure you get it right is to cut the above text and paste it directly into the Custom options box, replace everything there (take a backup of it first and put it in your firewall journal), and then customize it as needed with your device and subnet IPs.

CHAPTER 16
KEEPING GOOD RECORDS

Pfsense does a great job of tracking changes to its configuration, which you can view at **Diagnostics / Backup & Restore / Config History**. While this log answers the question of what changed, it does not answer the question of "why?"

For this reason, I recommend a simple log, kept in Notes for Apple users or Notepad for Windows users, of any changes you make to the configuration of your firewall. You don't need to go into all the details of what you changed if you can summarize it in the text, but it is important to explain why you made the change you did. This will be invaluable down the road when you are trying to troubleshoot an issue as it answers the question, "What was I thinking?" when you made a particular change.

As these recipes show, pfSense is a powerful security appliance with a myriad of configuration options, most of which we did not even touch in this book. For this reason, keeping a change journal is invaluable, especially if what you have learned so far leads you to further experimentation.

Form good habits now, before you need them because someday you will be thankful you made that journal entry when you are months or years down the road and don't have a clue what you changed or why.

CHAPTER 17
BACKUPS, JUST IN CASE

This recipe will describe how and why to make regular backups of your firewall configuration and how to restore them if something goes wrong with a change you have made.

pfSense has built into it the ability to create and store automatic backups on Netgate's servers whenever a change is made on your firewall. For maximum protection in the event of a failure, I recommend taking advantage of the online backup capabilities and manually making backups you store on your local system. The reason that you need both is that in the event of a failure that causes you to lose your internet connection, you are going to need those local backups to restore your firewall, as you likely won't be able to get access to the online backups from where you are.

LOCAL BACKUP FIRST

Making a backup whenever you make a significant change to your firewall configuration (and documenting that change per "Chapter 16 - Keeping good records") makes reverting in case the change causes problems both quick and easy.

Go to **Diagnostics / Backup & Restore to set up the local backup**. Under Backup Configuration, enter:

- Set **Backup area** to "All".
- Uncheck **Skip packages**.
- Check **Skip RRD data**.
- Click the blue **Download configuration as XML** button and an XML text file will be downloaded to your PC.

You can restore a backup from this same page by going to the Restore Backup section and specifying the name of the XML backup file by clicking **Choose File** next to **Configuration file**.

As long as you are storing the backup files on your local PC, I generally don't recommend encrypting them unless you are concerned about who has access to the files or your network.

Note that these backups you are making are for disaster recovery purposes. You would use them in case you ever need to wipe and restore your pfSense firewall or if your firewall device fails and you need to make/purchase a new one. pfSense itself is also making backups of the firewall as you make changes to your configuration.

If you go to **Diagnostics / Backup & Restore / Config History**, you will see that pfSense records all changes to the configuration as you make them and allows you to restore that configuration at a specific point in time. You can also determine the differences between two sets of changes by using the **Diff** button, as the instructions on the page describe.

ONLINE BACKUPS

Starting with version 2.4.4 of pfSense, the core software includes the ability to make automatic online backups. The Automatic Configuration Backup (ACB) service in pfSense will automatically encrypt and upload the configuration to Netgate servers whenever a change is made. Only the most recent 100 configurations are kept, however, that should be plenty.

To set up the ACB service, go to **Services / Auto Config Backup / Settings**, and then enter:

- Click the **Enable ACB** checkbox.
- Generate a complex password (and store it securely on your end) using whatever method works best for you and enter it into the **Encryption Password** field.
- Enter a name to identify your backup series, in case you need to call Netgate to try and find your backups in the **Hint/Identifier** field.
- Click the blue **Save** button to save your configuration.

Your configurations will now be encrypted and saved to Netgate whenever you change your firewall's settings. The password for this encryption never leaves your firewall, so your information is secure on Netgate's server. By the same token, if you lose your password, Netgate cannot help you decrypt your online backups so be sure to save it somewhere safe!

Besides your password, you also need to save the firewall's

Device Key. This is the unique identifier for your firewall that links the online backup back to your device. If you ever rebuild your firewall from scratch, you will need to reenter the Device key to access your online backups. You can find this value through **Services / Auto Configuration Backup / Restore**. Write it down and keep it safe!

To restore an online backup, go to **Services / Auto Configuration Backup / Restore.** Providing your device key is entered, you will see all the online backups available for your device. Click the blue down arrow icon to the right of each backup entry to see the details on the changes for a particular backup. When you know the one you want to restore, click the blue circular arrow to start the restoration.

ONE FINAL WORD ON BACKUPS

One final word of warning: You need to make sure when you are restoring a backup that it is to the same model device as was used to make it. Restoring a backup between different Netgate® models or home-built firewalls with different specifications is likely to be problematic. You are rolling the dice on whether the restored device will work properly, depending on what the hardware differences are.

CHAPTER 18
UPDATE PFSENSE

K eeping your devices patched and up to date is one of the most important things you can do to protect the security of any environment. As I discussed in "Chapter 9 - Isolate your IoT", the inability to patch most IoT devices is one of the primary reasons why they are such a risk to both businesses and individuals who attach them to their home or company networks.

Unlike the terrible patching and security record of many consumer routers, pfSense is a commercial product that starts out secure by design and is updated regularly to patch flaws and vulnerabilities discovered in the product. All software products have vulnerabilities, which should not be considered a strike against them. What matters is how diligent the company or group behind the software is in patching these promptly.

Updating your pfSense is as simple as going to **System / Update**. This page will show you the current status of your pfSense software and whether an update is available. If the **Status** shows as "Up to date", you're all good. You can also view whether an update is available from the pfSense dashboard. The System Information box will show if an update is available.

If an update is available, ensure you have a current backup as described in "Chapter 17 - Backups, just in case". Also, be sure to go to the Netgate website and read the release notes for the update in case there are actions you need to take before or after the upgrade to ensure its success.

To start the update, click the blue checkmark. The update will be downloaded, and your router will likely reboot, so plan on this downtime before starting.

In addition to the pfSense firewall itself, you should periodically check your installed packages to see if any updates are available. To do so, go to **System / Package Manager,** which will display the Installed Packages page.

If a newer version of a package is available than the one currently installed, the Version column will be highlighted, stating the old and new versions. To update, click the update icon (two arrows in a circle) on the right of the package. Click the green **Confirm** checkbox that will appear next to start the update. Repeat this for each package needing an update.

I suggest checking your firewall and packages monthly to see if updates are available. When both pfSense and package updates are available, upgrade pfSense first before upgrading the packages, as the package updates may depend on new functionality in the pfSense update. Check the release notes to be sure.

CHAPTER 19
A REALITY CHECK

P fSense is an excellent firewall with many great features, but even if you implement all the recipes I have discussed in this book, this alone is not enough to guarantee the security of your home or small business network. For that matter, nothing guarantees security in today's world of constantly evolving threats and technologies.

However, that is not a reason to give up. Just as with safety measures on cars, each measure by itself may do little to prevent accidents or injury, however when combined, they protect drivers and passengers far better than the cars of 20 years ago.

Likewise, your security program needs to be considered in terms of layers of protection at:

- The user layer
- The network layer
- The application layer
- The OS layer

- The device layer

While this book has discussed the network layer and how to leverage pfSense to improve it, the protections you implement at the other layers are equally important. While this book is not intended to address the full security stack, here are just a few questions you should consider to improve each of your security layers.

THE USER LAYER

- Do your users (home or small business) understand how to spot phishing threats?
- Do your users understand what malware is and how to spot potential threats in email?
- Do your users understand why they should never plug USB sticks into the PCs or electronic devices into their networks that have not been authorized?
- Do your users understand what social engineering attacks are and how to spot them?
- Have you educated your users on how to make and use good passwords?
- Do your users know whom to call if they have or suspect a problem?

THE NETWORK LAYER

This book, enough said...

THE APPLICATION LAYER

- Do your users understand the need only to use authorized software on their PCs or mobile devices?
- Do your users understand the dangers of "cracked" and stolen software they can download online?
- Are you keeping your applications up to date against the latest vulnerabilities by periodically checking for and applying patches?

THE OS LAYER

- Have you configured the operating system (OS) on your devices to use all the security features available?
- Are you keeping your device operating systems up to date against the latest vulnerabilities by periodically checking for and applying patches?
- Have you enabled automated updating of operating systems wherever it is available?

THE DEVICE LAYER

- Are you backing up the data on your devices regularly?
- Have you enabled encryption on your devices where it is available?
- Do you have a record of all the devices in your environment, including serial numbers and who they are assigned to?

- Do you understand how to dispose of your devices securely, including erasing or destroying all sensitive data that they may contain?

AFTERWORD

I hope you have enjoyed this book and its recipes. If you implement all of them, your internet security and that of your family or small business will be significantly enhanced, especially compared to a consumer-grade router or WiFi access point.

Even if you did not implement all the recipes, just having a pfSense appliance as your edge router will significantly advance in terms of pure security (a stateful firewall) and performance for your local network. Enjoy and stay safe online!

ABOUT THE AUTHOR

Michael Lines is a seasoned information security and risk executive with 25 years of experience, including multiple roles as Chief Information Security Officer (CISO) for international organizations. He has also led advisory Information Security practices, assisting companies in managing risk and achieving regulatory compliance. In this book, Michael provides a guide to consumers and small businesses on how they can reduce their exposure to internet threats by leveraging the pfSense firewall.

in linkedin.com/in/michaellines